To Kathleen,

Best Wishes,

Kenny Bell   6-10-2020

Jimmie Davis
More Than Sunshine

by Kenny Gill

edited by Robert Gentry and Patricia Martinez

ISBN 1-893693-07-4
Copyright © 2000

Visit the Kenny Gill homepage website
www.kennygill.com

Published by
Sweet Dreams Publishing Company
P.O. Box 850 ~ Many, LA 71449
Ph. (318) 256-3495 FAX (318) 256-9151
www.sweetdreamspub.com

PRINTED IN THE UNITED STATES OF AMERICA

JIMMIE DAVIS

MORE THAN SUNSHINE

BY

KENNY GILL

FORWARD

Kenny Gill has performed and recorded with over 65 major artists. He has performed on many TV and radio shows across the country including the Louisiana Hayride and the Grand Ole Opry. In 1997, the great state of Louisiana honored him by his induction into the Louisiana Hall of Fame.

For more than 25 years, Kenny has been a close friend and played as guitarist for Governor Jimmie Davis. Kenny has written his memories of those 25 years of association with one of the most honored Governors in United States history.

You'll read stories that will make you laugh and make you cry. I envy Kenny for being able to be around one of the most profound American legends who has lived for more than a century, having celebrated his 100th birthday on September 11, 1999.

I hope you will enjoy reading these "special moments" in Kenny's life. Congratulations Kenny on your extraordinary career with the Governor as well as your continued success in country music.

Sincerely,

David McCormick, Prop.
ERNEST TUBB RECORD
SHOPS, INC.
Headquartered in Nashville, TN

ACKNOWLEDGEMENTS

I want to thank my wife Jeanene for helping me write this book. Furthermore, I want to thank her for the many hours of word processing and editing in making this venture a reality. Other deserving thanks go to Susie Labry, Governor Jimmie Davis and Mrs. Anna Davis, without whose help it would not have been possible to complete this book.

I would also like to thank my publisher, Sweet Dreams Publishing Co. of Many, LA. I want to thank Robert Gentry and Patricia Martinez for editing the book and to Martha Bass for doing the production on the book.

Kenny Gill

TABLE OF CONTENTS

An Introduction to
Jimmie Davis

Jimmie Davis was one of the 11 children born to Sam Jones Davis and Elizabeth Works Davis. The family lived in a two-room cabin in the small farming community of Beech Springs, Jackson Parish, LA.

The Davis family were tenant farmers. They provided the labor. The landowner provided the land, the seed, the mules and the equipment necessary to work the land. Farming "on the halves," the family received half the proceeds of the cotton crop produced. The life was hard. The day began for the Davis children before the sun rose. Breakfast was a simple but hardy meal of biscuits, syrup, bacon and lots of flour gravy. Then everyone went off to the fields to begin the task of picking cotton.

Mother Davis left the field a little earlier than the rest of the family to fix dinner, a meal we now call lunch.

Like breakfast, the meal consisted of staples readily available to the family: cornbread, peas, greens, maybe a rabbit or a squirrel and on special occasions, a potato pie.

Then it was back to the cotton field and after 14 hours the family packed it in. Jimmie wrote, "We washed our feet in a big tub every night. On Saturday we all got a full bath. The first one in got a really good bath. The last one got a mud bath."

Papa Davis would read scriptures quickly because the young ones dozed and nodded off to sleep knowing that four o'clock the next morning would come all too quickly.

Jimmie remembers a conversation between a stranger and Sam Jones Davis. The newcomer asked Jones how he made a living. With a wry grin the weather-beaten Jones responded, "Make a living, mister we don't try to make anything. We just try to survive."

But never-the-less, Jimmie's memories are all positive and warm. He writes, "People have asked me what it felt like growing up and I tell them that it was like one great, continuous party. We enjoyed each other and we had something going on all the time. We had companionship and we had a certain amount of excitement.

"But most of all, what we had was love," he said.

Northeast Louisiana, insignificant by many measurements, is the spawning ground of Louisiana's political leaders. Jackson Parish, along with Caldwell Parish to the east and Winn Parish to the south, has provided the State of Louisiana with no less than five governors and countless senators, congressmen and many other political leaders.

Aspiring to a better life, young Davis attended Louisiana College at Pineville, LA and later Louisiana State University (LSU) at Baton

Rouge, LA, majoring in education with a minor in psychology. He waited on tables in school cafeterias. He sang on the street corners of Baton Rouge and Alexandria, LA to his own guitar accompaniment, earning money to pay for his education. But sometimes even this was not enough.

He interrupted his education to return to Jackson Parish and sharecrop once again to get money to continue.

When he graduated from LSU, Jimmie embarked on a career that would span teaching, music, politics and business. He has been a resounding success at all of them.

Jimmie has written some 700 songs. His <u>You Are My Sunshine,</u> the official song of the State of Louisiana, has been published in more than 30 languages and has been recorded by many popular music artist. It has been broadcast on national radio and television more than three million times.

He entered politics with his appointment to the Clerk of City Court of Shreveport, LA and began a journey that culminated in two successful campaigns for the highest office that the State of Louisiana can confer on anyone — the governorship.

His first term as governor from 1944 until 1948 was a progressive one and a model of fiscal responsibility.

He took action to revive the state's forestry industry, ravaged in the 1920's and 1930's by unwise harvesting tactics that denuded much of the state's acreage. Trees were cut without regard for replanting and by the '40's much of the formerly fertile forestlands were wastelands. His administration passed the Forestry Act and today the state grows more timber than it can cut.

He also started the first state employees retirement system, the first step toward developing a cadre of trained and professional employees.

Drivers were licensed for the first time in Louisiana. Today Jimmie still holds Louisiana drivers license number one.

When he left office in 1948, there was a comfortable surplus in the state treasury that was used by future administrations to fund the state's first old-age pension program.

His efforts at industrial development generated more jobs during a single four-year period than at any other time in LA history.

When Jimmie served as governor the second time, from 1960 until 1964, Louisiana suffered the worst problems in the state's history since reconstruction.

A nationwide recession plunged Louisiana into a deficit situation. Concurrent with this, the state was chosen by the federal government as the deepest of the deep South states for the integration of its elementary schools.

The state's financial problems were solved when Jimmie proposed to the Legislature a budget that was actually lower than the one of the proceeding year. This had never been done before and has never been done since.

The knotty problem of desegregation was solved, as Jimmie had promised in his inaugural address of 1960 "without prejudice and without violence."

While other Southern states were holding funerals for victims of racial violence, Louisiana underwent this social change seamlessly. "We didn't even have a fistfight," Jimmie recalled.

Jimmie served as governor for two terms — eight years — and never raised taxes. No other governor — before or after — can make this claim.

It is doubtful if Jimmie Davis will ever be given credit for the many good things he has done. A great deal of this is of his own doing.

Slow to anger, quick to smile and praise, he keeps his own counsel. He does not brag or boast. As a consequence, the story of his administrations has been told in headlines and television and news clips. These accounts are rarely flattering and are often inaccurate.

But this has not concerned Jimmie Davis.

He believes within himself that history will judge him accurately for his works and when the moving finger has written, it will record that he has accounted well for his stewardship as a public official, as a personality and as one of God's creatures.

He has an abiding and unshakable belief in the hereafter. He has explained it in his book and song entitled, *Louisiana, This One's For You.*

He says: "...Guess I'll stay here 'til it's all over, then back at Beech Springs, where they'll lay me down.

"I will arise on that great morning. I'll put on my robe and my starry crown."

It is hard to explain Jimmie Davis to anyone who has never really spent a lot of time with him. There is a tendency to stereotype him. His success in entertainment makes it difficult for some to appreciate the depth of the man.

They ask: "Why does Jimmie Davis endure while others fade away?"

They overlook his obvious academic qualifications (with a master's degree, he is one of the best-educated men to occupy the office of governor); they ignore his achievements as governor of Louisiana (his was the only administration in Louisiana history to reduce spending one year from the previous one, never equaled before or since), they underestimate his staying power (when others who occupied the governor's office have been relegated to obscurity and near-oblivion, he still tours the country, performing for a grateful constituency).

When the complete history of Louisiana has been written, there will be a prominent place for Jimmie Davis. He will warrant much more than a footnote. The account will note his obvious talent and the remarkable career, which grows even more remarkable with each passing day. It will call attention to the unique contributions he has made to his native state.

He is a remarkable man who has been confidante of presidents; co-star of movie personalities; co-performer of musical genius and counselor to scores of public officials who have sought his advice.

But he has never forgotten that he was humbly born the son of a sharecropper. The glow of success has never dimmed that humility; the roar of the crowd has never overpowered it. He has never forgotten it. He carries it with him always.

Jimmie Davis is, essentially, a humble man. And that is why Jimmie Davis endures.

Jimmie Davis: living and enduring proof that nice guys don't always finish last.

---Ed Reed

INTRODUCTION OF
YOU ARE MY SUNSHINE
USED BY GOV. JIMMIE DAVIS

I was with three other musicians a long time ago, we were barn-storming the country trying to make a little dough,

We made all the chili joints eating hotdogs and stews, and at night time three deep in a four bit bed all singing the hard time blues,

Hoping someday we'd make a hit and things would be sweet, then we'd settle down on that place they call easy street,

And so it happened on one July the 6th, we recorded a little ditty and it went something like this........

"You Are My Sunshine"

-Jimmie Davis

MY GUITAR

I suppose I can't remember when I didn't play guitar or at least wanted to play guitar. I remember when I was six years old my mother would take me over to her mother's house, my grandmother and my first cousin, who lived with my grandmother, had an old guitar with about three or four strings on it. He was a couple of years older than I was. I crawled under the bed and grabbed that old guitar and tried to plunk on it a little bit at six years old. When he caught me he would beat the tar out of me, but I wanted to play it. So the minute he was out of sight, I would grab it again. I continued to play his guitar when I could, because, of course, I didn't have one at home.

So I improvised by making one with a cigar box and a couple of wires out of the screen door at home. When my mother found out that I pulled wires out of the screen door to make a guitar, she whipped me pretty good. It was almost unplayable, it just made a little fleeting noise. I was kind of satisfied with it.

Then by the time I was eight years old, I'd become friends with a young boy up the street by the name of Jerry Payne. His mother, who was a real sweet lady, played to my estimation fantastic guitar. She probably just played a few chords just to satisfy herself. She had a nice Gibson guitar. Under her bed was an old guitar. So when I saw that guitar, I pulled it out and started picking with it. She mentioned that she may want to sell that guitar to me.

My birthday was coming up January 7, and I told Dad that I had seen a little army truck at one of the furniture stores on Main Street in my hometown of Bunkie, LA and that I wanted that little truck for my birthday, until I saw this guitar. That little truck was about a dollar and a half to about two dollars, and she wanted six dollars for the guitar. Six dollars was about half a week's pay for my dad. He made about $12 a week at the time. We weren't very affluent, and Dad told me at the time, "I'll try to get it for you, but I don't promise." Well, he did. He got that guitar for me and I started playing on my own. I just loved finding new chords and new adventures, so to speak on the guitar. It was just an absolutely magical time for me.

———◆———

MY TWO LOVES

From early childhood there were basically two loves in my life, one was playing the guitar and the other was airplanes. I just absolutely loved airplanes. When I could, I'd get my dad to take me to a little grass strip right outside of town to look at airplanes and go up and touch them, and that was just a magical time for me. But I knew that I would probably never own or fly a real airplane, so I built model airplanes for many years and enjoyed them quit a bit. I would enter contests and really enjoyed this time in my life.

But guitar was always the most important thing to me. At about the age of seven I was playing a few chords on guitar and had never had any lessons. This was about 1943.

ON THE CAMPAIGN TRAIL

I had heard that Jimmie Davis and his band were coming to town on the campaign trail running for Governor for the State of Louisiana. So, I asked my dad, when he came home from work, "Please take me to town to see Governor Jimmie Davis." This was in the late fall of 1943. I had never heard a real band play.

He was set up with his band on the depot platform on the Main Street of Bunkie. The platform was about four or five feet high off the ground and I was right up against the depot platform looking straight up at Jimmie Davis and his band. It was the most magnificent, terrific, tremendous band that I could have imagined! It was just unbelievable to me at seven years old.

Like I said, I had never really heard a real band play, so, any band would have been terrific to me, but these guys were good. In fact the fiddle player in the band was Johnny Gimble. Today he is very famous all over the country and he has become a friend of mine.

So I definitely knew who Jimmie Davis was. To me he was 40 feet tall. He had starred in two or three movies which I saw at the local movie theater. The movies were *Louisiana* and the other was *Mississippi Rhythm*. But I had seen Jimmie in some bit parts with Jimmy Wakely, another "B" western movie cowboy. To me Jimmy Davis is the epitome of success in music. The man is just a giant.

19

---◆---

"Still Pickin"

I have continued to play music to this day. In the past, I worked day jobs to support myself and played music at night. I made as much playing music in one night as I did all week long working manual labor, but I never gave up my day job. I always tried to keep a day job for security.

---◆---

My Times With Governor Jimmie Davis

This story is not about me, but about *my time with Jimmie Davis*. It wasn't until about 1963 that I actually performed with Jimmie and that was at a fund raising event that took place at Istrouma High School in Baton Rouge. Jimmie and the gospel quartet, The Plainsmen, were going to play, and somebody asked me to play there. It was a benefit for C.B. Cutrer, who was dying of cancer. And that night, I saw the Governor there. He didn't know who I was, but I certainly knew who he was. He asked me if I would play guitar with him. Apparently, somebody told him that I was a good guitar player. I played guitar with him and it went just great and I really enjoyed it!

From time to time I saw him at the Governor's Mansion in Baton Rouge, as I was invited by his son, Little Jimmie we called him, to come over and pick a little bit with him, because Little Jimmie played guitar and also played drums. When I was in the mansion several times, Jimmie would walk in and he would see me there. So, I assumed he knew who I was. And of course, I was playing as I say "12" nights a week at that time so a lot of people knew me.

———◆———

THE STORE

I opened my retail music store in Baton Rouge in August of 1965. One day I got a phone call from Governor Davis. He wanted to know if I had some item he needed. I said, "Why certainly, Governor." I said, "Come right on over," and he did. He always had a friend with him and one of the friends was Don Murry, his pilot. Don had given me flying lessons before I became a pilot.

The Governor was in my store one day and we began talking about good guitar pickers, and he says, "You know, Kenny, I never played too much guitar." And that day the Governor gave me one of the biggest compliments I had ever had!

He said, "To play guitar like you do, Kenny, you got to woodshed it." Now to people who might not know what he was referring to, it means that you have to put in a lot of time practicing. I did, I put a lot of time in learning to play. Not having any lessons, it took quite a bit longer to learn.

When I was a kid, we were too poor to pay for lessons. It was ridiculous even to give that a thought, so I had to learn on my own.

When I found somebody who could play better than I did and that was every time I turned around, then I made friends with him right quick and asked him how to do this and how to do that and so that's how I learned to play. It was long and tedious to learn to play. Anybody can play guitar, but it takes a technician to become an accomplished guitarist. I hope that I am at this point, because after playing guitar for 57 years as of 2000, that's a lot of picking and a lot of learning. That was a compliment from Jimmie, it really was! That was in the late '60's.

---◆---

PLAYING WITH JIMMIE DAVIS

I was playing in the early 1970's with Joe Lamedola, a Dixieland trumpet player and a very good one. He had a Dixieland group in Baton Rouge. He told me that we were invited to play for the opening of American Bank's new building downtown. So, we played there for three nights and on the second night I was there, unbeknownst to me, Governor Davis walks in with his lovely wife, Anna, who by the way is a real sweet lady.

He looked up at me and I nodded hello to him and on the break I went over to him and I just happened to have my camera with me.

I told him, "Governor, could I take a picture with you?"

He said, "Oh, by all means." He was very cordial. He always is.

And so we took several pictures of us and with, I call her, "Miss Anna."

He said to me that night, "Kenny, are you playing anywhere tomorrow morning?"

I said, "Well, I don't know, Governor, what do you have in mind?"

He said, "Well, we're going to play out here in front of the bank as part of the grand opening. Would you like to play with me?"

I said, "I certainly would." That was in 1973.

From then on, he would call me to play jobs with him. I played with Jimmie Davis fairly regularly to this date more than 25 years later. In the mean time I had my own group and I played music engagements in between playing with Jimmie Davis. He continued to hire me to play with him, and so we grew very close. We became best of friends and becoming very best of friends he has given me many, many moments of happiness, many moments of laughter and enjoyment. His lovely wife, Anna, is an absolutely perfect match for Jimmie.

---◆---

AT THE TABERNACLE

Jimmie's wife, Anna is one of the original members of the Chuck

Wagon Gang, a gospel singing group headquartered in Ft. Worth, TX. I'm very familiar with them, because as a boy I used to really like to listen to their music and still do. I eventually played a couple of engagements with them at the Jimmie Davis Homecoming in Jonesboro, LA which takes place every first Sunday of each October and it is a beautiful experience.

There's a little church service that morning at 10 o'clock. Then we have dinner on the grounds, then we pick and sing till around 2:30 or 3:00 and have prayer and go home.

It's very inspirational. There's probably three to five thousand people there each year. Under these big tall pine trees there's a band-stand and we have a real nice time together.

———◆———

THE STORYTELLER

I suppose Jimmie Davis can deliver one of his stories better than anyone else. I could never deliver a story like he can. All the stories he tells of his childhood are in the book called *You Are My Sunshine*, and I urge you to get a copy and read the book. The book is really good.

Things have happened along life's highway with us, especially between Jimmie and me. These are things that I will never ever forget and these memories with Jimmie have warmed my heart many times. I have a tremendous respect for Jimmie Davis. He is probably one of the most dependable people I've ever known, and the most modest person I've ever known. He's very sincere in everything he does and everything he says. Everywhere we go everybody loves him. Everybody knows him or wants to know him.

Someone will come up to him that hasn't seen him in many years and they may say, "Why, Jimmie, you remember me? Well, I'm so and so from so and so, and I knew you when you were Governor in so and so year." And if Jimmie doesn't know them, which is rare because he does remember almost everybody, but if he doesn't know them he won't say, "I'm sorry I don't remember you." I've never heard him say that.

He will always leave them with a feeling of contentment, such as, "Yes, I knew Jimmie remembered me." That feeling would be transferred or said to this person in a way that makes him believe that maybe Jimmie does remember him, even if he doesn't. If he doesn't remember this Mr. John Doe, who's come up and shook his hand and patted him on the back Jimmie would say, "Sure, I remember you. You and I used to steal hogs together."

Now that makes this guy really feel good, believe it or not, because the people around him have heard Jimmie admit that he and Jimmie have been together before, when in fact Jimmie's never seen him in his life and doesn't remember him.

Jimmie has an excellent memory, he's very good about remembering names. Someone will come up to him that he hasn't seen in 40 years and he'll know their name, where they're from and what they do for a living or what they did for a living. He absolutely amazes me.

———— ◆ ————

JIMMIE, THE MAN

Jimmie is a very sentimental person. I've seen him cry many times on the bandstand. For instance we played an engagement in Grapeland, TX. There were 5,000 people in the audience and another 5,000 milling around. At that point in his life, he was 97, we had to help him around because his legs were very weak, but his mind was still sharp. When we finished playing they gave him a standing ovation and he broke down and started crying.

And it was a real sad thing for me, because..., I kinda know how he felt. I really do. I've not been fortunate enough to have 5,000 people stand up and cheer for me and probably never will, but I can only imagine how he must have felt.

And, of course, almost everywhere we go, he gets standing ovations and Miss Anna, I don't want to leave her out, because she is a great part of the Jimmie Davis Singers. She is right there with him all the time taking care of him and sees that everything is worked out for him. This was quite an occasion for him in Grapeland.

THE MCI BUS

We travel in a beautiful MCI bus that's owned and operated by Mr. A.J. Kent and his wife, Lillie. The bus was completely refurbished from the ground up by Mr. Kent, who is a gifted craftsman.

The bus is like a apartment on wheels. It has couches, chairs, color TV and a stove and shower, bathroom, beds, even a washing machine, if you want to wash some clothes. It has everything that you would have at home, including a telephone.

The Governor just loves to travel in this beautiful bus, because it makes things so convenient, and travel is so easy because we don't have to worry about where we're going or how to get there, because Mr. Kent has it all worked out before we get on the bus. The bus is absolutely trouble free.

We've played from the East Coast, through Toledo, Ohio, and all over to East and Central Texas and covered the entire coast down here, too, including Florida. So, we've traveled quit a lot with the Kents.

GETTING ON THE SERIOUS SIDE

Occasionally, Jimmie and I are on the bus when it is parked, just he and I alone, and he'll get pretty serious with me, like one time

27

before a show we were sitting there and I'm just reading through a magazine.

He tells me, "You know, Kenny, some people think I'm crazy to run these highways like this."

I said, "Well, Governor, I don't think you're crazy. I think you're doing something you like to do."

He said, "Yes, I am, because I just can't sit home in a rocking chair and let time go by. Kenny, I would rather die on the bandstand than die in a rocking chair."

Well, I said, "Governor, just keep doing it. That's what's keeping you going, so don't stop doing these performances that you do, and I'll be right there with you, too."

———◆———

GETTING ON WITH IT

I remember one time I was over at Jimmie's house helping him do something he'd ask me to do and as I sat there with him I said, "Now, Governor, let me ask you a serious question. You've had several political appointments or political jobs, such as Governor twice and Police Commissioner for the City of Shreveport. You've been Public Service Commissioner. You've made movies. You've written books, you've recorded dozens of music albums. You've done just about everything in the world. Tell me this, Governor, what is the most important thing in this life?"

And without hesitating one moment, he comes right back with, "Getting ready to die."

He surprised me when he said this. My first impression of that statement was, "Finances." I at first thought he meant getting his finances together for his son or his family before he dies and then I realized that wasn't what he was talking about. I felt ashamed of myself inwardly for thinking finances were what he was talking about, when in fact he was talking about getting right with his Maker before he died. It didn't take him a half a second to tell me that. He just came right back with it. Jimmie's a good man.

———◆———

A NEW PAIR OF BOOTS

Recently a Hollywood movie was released named "Blaze" that depicted the life of former Governor Earl Long of Louisiana and his mistress Blaze Star.

One afternoon Governor Davis stopped by my office for a visit and informed me that he and Miss Anna had just seen the movie "Blaze".

I asked him how he enjoyed it and he commented that "it had quite a bit of Hollywood fiction in it and some of the dialogue was misquoted." I agreed with him, as I had seen the movie and had worked closely with Governor Long until his death.

I asked if there was anything that really impressed him in the movie and he said he "enjoyed the movie quite a bit." He said he was impressed with one scene so much that after the movie he went out and bought a new pair of boots!

———◆———

I WOULDN'T CHANGE A THING

On another musical engagement trip somewhere while we were alone together in the bus, I asked him, "Governor, after doing all that you have done in life, if you had it to do all over again, would you change anything?"

He answered, "Nope, not a thing." That kind of surprised me too!

———◆———

HONESTY

You know, musicians have always been noted for not having enough money or somehow needing money. But from the first job I played with Jimmie Davis 25 years ago, I would never ask for the pay. I just went back to my office to continue to run my business because I felt in my heart that he was an honest and sincere person.

In two days, there was a check in the mail for me, and today it's still the same way. After each musical engagement, I took pleasure in saying thanks to him and shaking his hand and saying, "Governor, enjoyed it much."

And he always says, "Now, Brother Gill, I enjoyed it, too. I had a good time."

I said, "Yes, Sir, we sure did."

I always leave him with, "Governor, if you find work, write."

And he says, "I'll do better than that, I'll come see you."

That's always our final words, and you can bet within a couple of days I got a check in the mail. Jimmie's always been very good about that. I've never asked him for a dime. I've never had to. He's always done what he was supposed to do and, of course, by the same token, I treat him with great respect, because I do have great respect for him and Miss Anna both.

We have a wonderful, warm relationship, but I've known band leaders who may abscond with the funds and nobody gets paid. That has never and will never happen with Jimmie Davis, because he's a very honest person.

Traveling in Style with the Best

I can truly say the single greatest experience in my musical career has been my time with the Jimmie Davis entourage, because everywhere we go we're treated with utmost respect by everyone. No matter where we go, it's all red carpet treatment with Jimmie. We stay in good motels. And of course we eat the best foods. Everybody knows him, everybody loves him and he never meets a stranger.

Right at Home

We were in a little motel in Arkansas and Jimmie had just finished breakfast that morning. When walking out of the cafe he saw a table of men who looked like farmers having coffee and biscuits.

He left our table and went right over to them and started shaking their hands. Of course, he wasn't running for office, so there was really no reason for him to do that. But that's the kind of person he is. He's very friendly.

Overcoming Obstacles

He recently fell down in his bedroom and struck the back of his right hand on something sharp and cut the back of his right hand from his wrist to his ring finger. He just gouged out a terrible cut in his hand and suffered with it for a couple of days before Miss Anna made him got to the doctor.

When he finally went to the doctor, they fussed at him for not coming in earlier and they sewed the wound up and it took 11 stitches.

That was on Wednesday and we had to be in some little town 400 miles away that Saturday night for an engagement. He told us, "Well, I don't know how in the world I'm going to be able to sign these autographs, but I'm going to try to do it." When we perform we usually start the show around 7 p.m. to maybe 8 p.m. and then after that he'll go and do what we call "sit at his table," which is a folding table that's set up near the bandstand where he sells his records, tapes, CD's and books, etc.

I saw him sit at that table and shake every hand of the fans that came around which was a total of approximately 700 people comprising a line of two and three abreast for almost a block long waiting for autographs and handshakes.

He sat there until about 10:30 or 11 o'clock that night. He also signed autographs. He's a real sincere person and he loves people. He loves to talk to people, especially, country people. He loves to talk farming and hunting with them, because he used to hunt quite a bit. He really gets a charge out of that.

33

AT THE STORE

Once I had a retail store down on Government Street in Baton Rouge. Jimmie was in there one day standing around chatting with me. Most people who came into the store were young musicians and they may not have known who he is.

A black customer walked up to me and started telling me he wanted to buy a certain item.

He said, "I'd sure like to buy this from you, but my wife has taken all my money and I just can't buy it. Maybe next week when I get paid, I'll be able to do it. You know how those women are."

And Jimmie Davis, says, "Yeah, you gotta watch 'em."

This black guy had no idea who Governor Davis was. He pops back with, "Yeah, you ain't never lied, Daddy," and as he walked out of the store we just exploded with laughter.

CHRISTMAS PARTY GUESTS

We have our annual Christmas party at our home each year and we invited Jimmie and Miss Anna over. A friend of mine came in with his wife and other guests. A lady from upstate New York was with him. The lady was chatting with various people and then I saw her sitting down next to the Governor in front of the fireplace having a lengthy conversation with him.

I thought to myself, "Well, she must have found out who he is, and so she's going to gather as much information from him as she can."

The night went on and the party ended. Everybody went home.

So, I saw my friend a few weeks later. He said, "You know, we had a good time at that party. You remember the lady that was with me?"

I said, "Well, I saw her, yes."

He said, "Well, she's from up north and she told me after the party that she met the most interesting ol' gentleman and they sat and talked about an hour. He was very interesting and just as sweet as could be and had more little stories to tell her. They were so funny!"

And my friend told her, "Do you know who that was that you were talking to?"

She said, "No, I have no idea. Was that Mr. Gill's father?"

He said, "No, that was former Governor Jimmie Davis."

She had no idea who she was talking to. That's the kind of things we run into all the time, especially on the road, where people sometime have no idea who they're talking to.

He'll just treat them like they're very important to him. He's just a very sincere "one of us" kind of person.

———◆———

WHAT A LOAD!

Jimmie said that in the old days the only way they had to travel from engagement to engagement was in an old car. They put a luggage rack on top of the car. They put the bass fiddle up there and the suitcases and everything else and hoped it didn't rain.

He told me that one time they were coming through this little town and they turned a corner too fast and, "The bass fiddle flew off, suitcases flew off all over the street, and there were underclothes, hair tonic, Vicks Salve and Quinine scattered all over the street!"

———◆———

COURTING

Jimmie told me that after his first wife, Alvern, had sadly passed away, and that after a short period of time he dated a few ladies around Baton Rouge. One of the ladies he was dating was quite a bit younger than him.

They had been dating for several months when she came to him one day and said, "Jimmie, I think we ought to get married."

Jimmie replied, "Well, Honey, I don't think that would work out too good."

She asked, "Well, why not? I don't understand?"

He answered, "Well, there's a lot of difference in our ages and if you and I got married, after two or three years, you'll want to go out and do some fancy dancing, that wouldn't work, because I'd have to have you stay home and rub my back with Sloan's liniment."

————◆————

A FIRST-TIME NEW EXPERIENCE

One day I received a phone call from the Governor. He said, "Kenny, this is Jimma (as the Governor pronounces it) Davis. What are you doing this coming Tuesday at noon?"

I said, "Nothing in particular, Governor. What do you have in mind?"

He said, "Well, we're having a little baked coon over here at the house for several friends of mine. Would you like to join us?"

37

I thought he was kidding. I said, "Yeah, sure, Governor, I'd love to do that. I appreciate that very much."

He says, "OK, well, be here about quarter to twelve Tuesday. We're going to have lunch together."

I said, "All right." So, I'm thinking well, he's kidding. He's not going to have any baked coon! I didn't know what he would have, but it wouldn't be baked coon, I was sure.

So, I arrived at his house and there were three or four very distinguished politicians and businessmen from the community with the Governor and myself. No ladies, just men. After a short time, we were seated at the table and the cook brought out a big platter of baked coon. That's the first time I've ever eaten coon in my life.

And it sat there before me, and I said, "Well, I guess it's just as clean as pork." So I was served a portion of baked coon and ate it and it tasted just like roast pork to me. It was delicious! Nowhere in Baton Rouge would you find this, especially from a former Governor and especially sitting at his table eating baked coon in his home. That was an interesting little get together and he invited us to several others after that.

BONNARD BRONCO BUSTER

I have a friend in Castleberry, FL right outside of Orlando, who owns a foundry which produces beautiful bronzes, the Remington type, the Fisher type and many others. From time to time, I would buy a bronze from him and so I became friends with him over the telephone. His name is Henry Bonnard.

My middle son, Kirk, was planning to marry a young lady from Orlando and we were going to go to the wedding. I decided while I was in Orlando, I'd call Henry Bonnard, whose place of business was right outside Orlando. I called him and said I wanted to come by to see him while in Orlando. He told me, "Just let me know when you're in town and I'll send somebody to pick you up," and I did.

I went over to see Henry. He's a nice guy and has a beautiful place of business and sells beautiful articles in bronze. He mentioned to me that he really likes a particular singer from Louisiana and that he has all of his records.

I said, "Well, who is that?" He said, "Jimmie Davis."

I said, "Well, Henry, Jimmie's a very dear friend of mine. We play music together." Henry Bonnard was absolutely astonished. He couldn't believe it.

I said, "Yes, Jimmie and I have been playing together for a number of years, and we're very dear friends."

He said, "Well, I have admired Jimmie Davis all of my life, and I would like to do something for him." I said, "Well, that's fine. He'd appreciate whatever you want to do."

He said, "Will you tell the Governor when you get back to Baton Rouge that he can have any article in my store at no charge. The only thing I want you to do is take a picture of yourself presenting it to him, and I want to hang the picture in the store." I said, "Well, that's very nice of you, and I'll be glad to tell him."

So when I got back to Baton Rouge, I called him and said, "Governor, I want to come over to show you something." So, I went over to his house and brought the Bonnard catalog. I said, "There's a fellow in Florida that just absolutely thinks the world of you and owns a bronze casting company that produces Remington's reproductions and others. I said, "He's got hundreds and hundreds of them in stock of all kinds and he told me he wants to offer you one of anything in the store as a token of his admiration for you. You can have anything you want in his place."

The Governor said, "Well, my goodness, that's awful nice of him."

I said, "Well, he's a nice guy. He wants to give you something.

So, you take this catalog, look through it and decide what you want and then call and tell him."

So, a couple of days later, the Governor called me and said, "Kenny, that's awful nice of that fellow to do that, but I feel kinda funny about it." I said, "No, no, it's OK, because he wants to give it to you."

He said, "Well, I like this bronze by Remington called *Bronco Buster*. I think that will be a great choice."

I said, "OK, Governor. Here's his number. He has a 1-800 number. You give him a call and tell him who you are and tell him you appreciate what he's doing and he'll send it to you."

So, the Governor said, "OK." The Governor called the 1-800 number to Bonnard Bronze and Associates in Castlebery, FL and asked to speak to Henry Bonnard. Henry answers the phone and says, "This is Henry."

Jimmie said, "Mr. Bonnard, this is Jimma Davis. I'd like to talk to you about your bronzes. You wanted me to call you." He says, "Well, yeah, Jimmie."... At this point Mr. Bonnard doesn't realize that this is *The Jimmie Davis*, so, he says, "Jimmie, what can I do for you?"

Now, Jimmie being very modest is in a predicament. He is not going to say, "You said that you'd give me a bronze if I'd call you to

41

tell you which one I want." So, when Mr. Bonnard says, "Yeah, Jimmie, what can I do for you." Jimmie says, "Oh, I'm just calling to see how the weather is down there." Henry Bonnard says, "The weather's fine Jimmie." Jimmie says, "OK, thank you." And he hung up.

So a day or two later I called the Governor. I said, "Did you talk to Henry Bonnard?" He said, "Well, yeah, but he just asked me what I wanted. He apparently didn't know who I was."

I said, "Oh, my gosh!" So, I called Henry Bonnard. I said, "Henry, did you know that was Jimmie Davis talking to you the other day?" He said, "Oh, My God, was that *The Jimmie Davis* I was talking to?" I said, "Yes."

He said, "I'm so sorry. I didn't realize who he was," he said, "What's his number? I'll call him right now." I gave him the Governor's number. He called the Governor and they had a nice chat on the phone.

The Governor told him, "This is really nice of you to do this, and if you insist I'll take a *Bronco Buster* from Remington. So, Henry Bonnard sent the full size *Bronco Buster* by Remington, which is about two and a half feet high solid bronze to my office.

It weighed about 85 pounds, and I took it over to the Governor's house, snapped some pictures and sent them to Mr. Bonnard. Mr. Bonnard appreciated this very much.

AGELESS

Now, at this writing I'm 63 years old and the Governor is 100, so he's 37 years older than I am. On one occasion, we were playing somewhere and before a performance, I told him, "Governor, we've got a problem."

"Oh," he said, "What's that?" I said, "I was outside a minute ago, just before we went on stage, and a lady come up to me and said, 'Jimmie, I'd like for you to give me your autograph.'" I said, "Well, Ma'am, I'm not the Governor."

She said, "You're not?" I said, "No, Ma'am, there's the Governor siting right over there." She says, "Oh, I thought he was the guitar player."

And the Governor found that quite amusing.

IT'S TIME TO ORDER

We did a show near the panhandle of Texas one Saturday night; the next day (Sunday morning) we all met in the motel restaurant to have breakfast before we left. Now sitting at the table were myself, Jimmie, and Miss Anna, Jimmie's cousin and his wife and Mr. and Mrs. A. J. Kent.

As the waitress was taking the orders the cousin said, "Lady, when you get the bill bring it to me. I'm gonna pick up this tab."

A.J. Kent said, "No. You bring it to me, I'm going to pick up the tab. His money's no good."

The cousin said again, "Nope. Don't bring it to that man. He's got foreign money. Just bring the ticket to me. I'm going to pick up this breakfast."

A.J. Kent replied, "No, no, you just bring it to me, don't worry about him."

Miss Anna punches Jimmie with her right elbow and said, "No, Jimmie will pick up the tab, huh, Jimmie?"

Jimmie looks up and says, "I'll have grits."

———◆———

THE SINGER

Usually before each performance, we'll get into the bus or motel room generally around 3 o'clock and have a little rehearsal with myself, the Governor, Miss Anna, and James Wilson, our rhythm guitar player, and of course, our piano player, Gary Goss, is usually there listening in.

When we had gone through four or five songs, I started kinda singing along with them in the background. I noticed the Governor would look at me kind of funny every now and then. I didn't know what was on his mind.

So, finally he stopped the music and he said, "Kenny, you know, you play an awful lot of guitar, but please don't try to sing when we're rehearsing." So apparently, the Governor likes my picking better then he does my singing.

———————◆———————

COURAGEOUS

On one of our trips luckily, somebody had a camera on board as we were near some little South Louisiana town. We looked and there was a 12-foot alligator near the side of the highway. Jimmie wanted to get a close look and somebody grabbed the camera.

Jimmie got out of the bus and just walked up to the alligator and somebody had the camera ready. The alligator swung his tail towards Jimmie, which could have broken both of his legs and Jimmie jumped up in the air and the alligator's tail went right under his feet and missed him.

Somebody snapped the picture at the same time. So, Jimmie has that picture of him in mid-air approaching the alligator. The alligator decided he was not happy to see him, so to speak!

Jimmie loves dogs so I gave him a couple of Catahoula Currs. In his book are several stories about animals. I'm sure if you read the book, you would really enjoy the one about the donkey tied to the bull and another about the possum all covered with cotton and another about the cats and on and on. So, the book *You Are My Sunshine* about Jimmie Davis is very humorous reading. I enjoyed it very much.

———◆———

MAKING DO

Jimmie said he was on his first campaign for Governor down in South Louisiana. He didn't have his band with him and the crowd kept asking him to sing, *You Are My Sunshine.*

He said, "Well, I'd like to, but I don't have anybody to accompany me." And one of the people there on stage said, "Aww, why, we've got the greatest piano player in the world right here in this little town. She's won this award, she's been to this school and that school, and played in Russia and did this and did that! Why she can follow you in anything you want to sing."

Jimmie said, "Well, go fetch her and get her over here and let's see."

So, they found her and brought her over and set up the piano for her and Jimmie says, "She commenced to playing arpeggios up and down the scale. It sounded like a cat was running across the keyboard of the piano that had been shot in the behind with a load of shoe tacks."

Now, if you younger people don't know what shoe tacks are, in the old days there weren't many shoe repair centers or shoe shops, so when your shoe soles wore out, you went to the local hardware store and bought a pair of shoe soles and a pocket full of shoe tacks with it. You had to actually tack the new shoe sole over the old shoe sole with shoe tacks. And I thought that was real funny. It brought back memories.

---◆---

Don't Mess With Jimmie!

Jimmie was telling me that a few years back he was in Nashville on one of the streets after a recording session. He was looking in a store window somewhere off of Broadway and I guess at this time he must have been about 80-years-old.

A man came up behind him and stuck a gun in his back, or what seemed to be a gun and cussed him out and said, "You so and so, I'm going to kill you right here. Give me every dime you got."

Well, Jimmie didn't do anything, but take his elbow and jammed it into the guy's chest. The guy fell down and then ran away, and Jimmie just stood there watching him.

He wasn't a person to fool around with when he was a young

47

man, much less now that he is an old man.

———◆———

SINGING IDOL

You know, from time to time, he would drop in to see me at my office and it was always such a pleasure to have him come by and drink a Coca Cola with us and visit. From time to time he would tell me, "Well, I got a letter from Gene today [meaning Gene Autry]." Now, Gene Autry has always been somebody special to me, because as a child I loved to see his movies.

One day, Jimmie came by and he had a letter from Gene with him. I said, "Governor, would you mind if I read it?" He said, "No, you can read it." So I did.

I said, "Governor, would you mind if I get Gene's address from you and drop him a line and tell him how much I've admired him for years?" He said, "Oh, no, I wouldn't mind a bit." I said, "Do you think he'll answer the letter?" He said, "Sure, he'd answer the letter."

I said to myself, "No way is this man going to answer my letter." But I got Gene Autry's address and sat down with my secretary and wrote him a letter. That was around August 21st of that year. By August 24th or 25th I received a letter from Gene Autry.

He was very pleasant in the letter, appreciated my writing him and from time to time without overdoing anything, I'd drop him a line and he'd answer right back. But Gene Autry, like Jimmie Davis, was a very pleasant person to talk to and to be with.

———◆———

ON THE FARM

At one time I had purchased some acreage just right outside of Baton Rouge and cleared it and fenced it. I built a little Acadian cabin on it, with hand built furniture and an old fashioned fireplace. I had a few horses out in the back and I kept telling the Governor about the place and he wanted to see it.

So, one day I called him and said, "Governor, I'm going to pick you up Saturday morning around 7 or 8 o'clock and take you out to what we call the farm [which is actually not a farm, it's just acreage with a few horses] and I'm going to cook breakfast for you. He really liked that!

I picked him up and drove him out to the farm and fixed us breakfast. We sat there, just he and I, in this little Acadian cabin and had a good ol' country breakfast of biscuits and sausage and eggs and grits. It was really nice.

This was something that I really wish I would have had on videotape. Jimmie loves that kind of goings on. I will remember this occasion forever.

DUMB BULL

One day on a trip the Governor and I were sitting and talking and one thing led to another. He asked me if I ever heard of a dumb bull. I said, "No, Governor, I don't even know what it is. What is that?"

"Well," he said, "it's something we used to make when we were little kids. We would take an old hollow log, when we could find one, not too big, maybe six to ten inches in diameter. We'd cut one end off real square. Then we'd take some green cow hide." Green cow hide is cow hide that hasn't been cured. It's still soft, freshly off the cow and it's apt to shrink when you let it dry in the sun.

He continued, "We took some green cow hide, stretched it across the mouth of that log and tacked it on with shoe tacks, or thumb tacks or nails or whatever. And when that thing dries, it's like a drum. Then you take it and put a little hole right in the middle of the hide, put a pretty strong string through it with a knot behind it so it can't slip out, and you pull the string taut with one hand and take a wet rag and run up and down the string with the other hand. It makes the most God awful roaring that you've ever heard in your life; it sounds like a 1,200 pound lion."

So he was telling me that when he was Governor for the first time, he had a friend that was visiting them at the mansion and slept on the floor above him. So, one day Jimmie had gone to her bedroom and had placed the dumb bull under her bed without her knowing it. Around 11 or 12 that night, he pulled on the string and started running the wet rag up and down the string. This thing bellowed like a giant lion or like a big grizzly bear. It was incredible. It'd scare the tar out of you! Well, their guest came out of that room like a freight train. She was as white as a sheet and didn't know what the heck was going on so they all had a big laugh about it. That next morning at breakfast he said her hands were still shaking from that night before.

She said, "Governor, I've never been that scared in my whole life as I was last night, when you started making that noise with that funny looking thing."

That was something to laugh at, but it took Jimmie to tell it, and when he tells it, it's much funnier than when I tell it. That is the story of the dumb bull.

---◆---

A BIG ONE

Jimmie said that in the little community of Beech Springs where he's from, they had church service only once a month, because they didn't have a hired preacher and there were no preachers anywhere near enough to have a church service every Sunday. The church was a couple of miles down the road from where he was raised. He said that it was announced that the preacher was leaving the church but there was a new preacher coming in.

It was understood that the new preacher would be there within three weeks. So, it came time for them to go to the church service that Sunday to meet the new preacher. It so happened that there was a young boy that came to church there that was retarded and he'd sit on the front row and talk real loud.

So, that particular Sunday he and his "Pa" were on the front row of the church to greet the new preacher. Now, it turned out that the new preacher was a real tall fellow. He must have been about six and a half feet tall.

The new preacher came up to the pulpit, starts to welcome people, when the retarded boy told his dad real loud, "Gawwly, Paw, he's a big SOB, ain't he?" And the whole place just went bonkers, it was hilarious. But again, you have to have Jimmie to tell you the story for it to really be appreciated.

———◆———

PO' FOLKS

Jimmie Davis and I were both raised very poor and, of course, Jimmie was raised much poorer than I. He always uses a statement that I fully subscribe to.

His statement is, "Why, they can't ration a thing that I haven't done without."

I think there's a lot of truth in that statement, coming from him, because I know exactly what he means by that statement.

GOLF

One day, I was over at the Governor's house and there was a golf game on television and I just asked him, "Governor, have you ever played golf?"

He looked at me and says, "Well, one time." I said, "One time?" He said, "Yeah." I said, "What happened?"

"Well," he said, "I wasn't very good at it. I hit so many bad balls, there was a little pond right off the golf course, the water in the pond rose six inches. That was the end of my trying to play golf."

BIGGEST BLADDER

Knowing the poor conditions Jimmie Davis suffered during his childhood, I can well imagine the truth behind some of the sad but humorous stories he tells of those very lean years so long ago. One that comes to mind is the story he tells about the lean Christmases he witnessed as a young boy.

Being the son of a sharecropper with 11 children tended to present a problem especially at Christmastime. One story he told me was that as a young boy he remembers his Christmas gifts consisted of a plucked blackbird and a hog's bladder.

For those of you who do not understand the meaning of such gifts, you have to understand that when you're as poor as the Davises were in those days any gift was much appreciated. To be a little more understanding of these "strange" gifts you'd almost have to hear Jimmie tell the story. He said "Well, we cooked the plucked blackbird and ate it and was happy to have it. As for the hog bladder we blew it up with air and used it for a basketball."

Jimmie said, "First time I saw a real basketball, I was trying to figure out what kind of an animal would have a bladder that BIG!"

———◆———

JIMMIE DAVIS IS AN INSTITUTION

Jimmie Davis has always been an institution in my mind. I've known about him most of my life. The first time I ever laid my eyes on Jimmie is when he ran for Governor the first time in 1943. I've admired his abilities and I've admired his talents. The years that I performed with him have been especially gratifying, very amusing many times and very interesting. He's one hundred percent gentleman, he's a very modest person, he's an extremely dependable person and a very forgiving person. He understands life and he understands people. He's an all around good friend.

I suppose just about everything that can be written about Jimmie Davis has been written except my very personal feelings.

Jimmie Davis is not only an institution, he's also a legend and good friend. Furthermore, I want to say that I am thankful to have known him, worked with him, and cried and laughed with him. he and Miss Anna will be on my mind and in my heart all the days of my life.

———◆———

COUZAN DUDLEY J. LEBLANC

One of Governor Davis' closest political allies was State Senator Dudley J. LeBlanc of Louisiana. Aside from being a State Senator, Mr. LeBlanc was a very likeable and intelligent entrepreneur.

The inventor and patent holder of an elixir and miracle patent medicine called Hadacol, Mr. LeBlanc was often heard doing his own radio commercials that sometimes featured testimonials of people who used the product.

One day during a radio broadcast commercial/testimonial promoting his Hadacol he introduced a Mrs. Brown (an African American) to explain just how Hadacol helped her. The testimonial went something like this:

"Yessuh Mista Couzan Dud, thank you fur lettin me tell all da folks bout yo wonderful Hadacol. Fuh years I couldn't do no house-woik, couldn't cut mah yawd, couldn't even sweep my flo cuz mah stummuk bother me so much. But after takin only 14 bottle of yo wonderful Hadacol, now I feels so good I'll put me belly up against anybody."

———◆———

REHEARSAL TIME

Before each and every concert Governor Davis would always call a rehearsal at around 3 p.m. At this time he would hand each member of the musical group a handwritten program or list of songs to be played. Through the years I tried to collect as many of these as possible. The following are a few examples of his handwritten programs for the day.

Eb Coming Home
F To my mansion
G At The Crossing
Eb Someone To Care
F# Green Green Green
E Nobody's Darlin'
C Suppertime
F Circle
D Sunshine

Oak Grove, LA
March 14, 1998

Kenny
G Show me the way
F I know Him
F# Happened
Eb The Last Few Miles
F Buttermilk
D Suppertime
D Sunshine

Bogalousa, LA
February 4, 1995

Kenny
Ab Mansion on The Hill
Ab Once a Day
F To my mansion in sky
F# Makes No Difference Now
F Nobody's Darlin'
D Columbus Stockade
F My Mary
Eb The Last Few Miles
F# Shackles and Chains
Eb Dating a Memory
D Suppertime
D Sunshine

Toledo, Ohio
August 7, 1993

G Mansion on The Hill
Today I Started loving you
F River
F Makes No Difference Now
Just a Closer Walk
Ab Once a Day
D Columbus Stockade
F# Nobody's Darling
F# Shackles & Chains
F Green Green Grass
Bb I Can't Stop loving you
Eb The Last Few Miles
Db Saints
D Sunshine

New Orleans, LA
April 24, 1994

57

Lake Arthur

F River
G Clover Walk
E Someone To Care
F Happened
Eb The Last Mountain
F I Know Him
Bb Taller Than Trees
G Show Me The Way
Anna
F Buttermilk
D Suppertime
D Sunshine

Lake Arthur, LA
Saturday, June 17, 1995

Ab Mansion on the Hill
F - Makes no Difference
E - Someone To Care
F - To my mansion misty
Ab - Once a Day
F# Shackles and Chains
Eb The Last Few Miles
F - Green, Green, Grass
F - My Mary
D - Suppertime
D Sunshine

Waldo, FL
May 22, 1993

———◆———

CROWD GATHERS TO FETE
JIMMIE DAVIS AT 100

Finally, we were privileged to participate in a gala celebration in Baton Rouge, LA, for the 100th birthday celebration for our dear friend and mentor Governor Jimmie Davis on Friday, September 10, 1999.

The event was held at the Radisson Hotel Grand Ball Room where over 960 guests were present for the occasion. The party drew former

Governors as well as the current Governor and a few gubernatorial candidates.

Chairman and Mrs. Robert Gentry of Many, LA hosted this auspicious occasion. Gentry has been a friend of Governor and Mrs. Davis for many years and has been active in booking and promotion of country, bluegrass and gospel music shows in Northwest Louisiana for many years and has booked Governor and Mrs. Davis many times throughout the period.

The Master of Ceremonies for the evening was well-known author and political analyst Gus Weill of Baton Rouge.

Mrs. Burn Page, wife of the Pastor of First Baptist Church in Baton Rouge, gave the invocation.

Soprano songstress, Mickey Mangum of Alexandria, LA entertained the crowd with two beautiful songs. The Lewis Family of Lincolnton, Ga., longtime friends of the Davises entertained with good down home country and bluegrass music.

The height of the entertainment portion of the evening was when Governor Davis and the Jimmie Davis Singers performed. The group consists of Anna Davis, James Wilson, Gary Goss and Kenny Gill.

At 100 years of age, Jimmie Davis' voice is still strong and he was able to sing several of the Jimmie Davis favorites including *You Are My Sunshine.*

Jimmie has served as a politician, singer, history teacher, coach, movie star, author and has written over 800 songs and recorded more than 50 albums and made seven motion pictures.

Despite the strong political presence at the birthday party, the emphasis was on Davis' musical career.

Guests received a compact disc of several versions of *You Are My Sunshine* by Davis and other artists, compliments of PeerMusic.

As Governor Davis lived to see January 1, 2000, he has lived into three centuries. When asked to what he attributes his longevity, Davis answered, "Clean living and goat's milk."

The gala event was a night to be remembered and enjoyed by all. Well-known entertainers and guests from around the world were present to honor Governor Davis on his special event.

Proceeds generated by this event were donated to the Jimmie Davis Tabernacle Fund in Beech Spring, LA.

It was with much great personal pleasure and honor that I've been privileged to be part of the Jimmie Davis Singers group for 25 years. As I have mentioned before, there will always be fond and warm memories of my many years with Jimmie Davis.

Kenny and Jeanene Gill at Jimmie Davis' 100th Birthday Celebration.

Well known entertainer "Tugboat Jerry" with author Gill.

Kenny Gill and friend "Little Roy Lewis" enjoying chatting during the Governor's 100th Birthday party.

Good friend and Jimmie Davis fan Vester Crutchfield visiting with Gill.

Former Louisiana Governor Edwin Edwards, Governor Mike Foster of Louisiana and Gill.

The Jimmie Davis Singers performing at the gala event. Left to right are Anna Davis, the Governor, Ted Jones behind him, Kenny Gill and Gary Goss.

Kenny Gill is shown with Gov. Jimmie Davis in better times, 1985.

This picture was taken at a Baton Rouge, LA outdoor concert in 1975. Left to right are Joe Marretta, Governor Davis, Kenny Gill, Anna Davis and James Wilson.

This photo was taken at the Jimmie Davis Homecoming at Beech Springs, LA in 1976. Left to right are James Wilson, Anna Davis, Jimmie Davis, Kenny Gill and Gary Goss.

Kenny Gill and Gov. Davis at a concert in 1977. Gov. Davis autographed the picture, "My best to a great man, Kenny Gill."

Kenny Gill, right, is shown performing with the Chuck Wagon Gang in this 1984 photo. Left to right are, unidentified , Anna Carter Davis, Rose and Roy Carter.

The Jimmie Davis Singers are shown performing for the Louisiana Legislature in 1983. Left to right are Ted Jones, Gov. Davis, Anna Davis, James Wilson and Kenny Gill. Standing behind Anna is Gov. David Treen.

The Jimmie Davis group is shown following a performance at the New Orleans Jazz Festival in 1991. Left to right are Johnny Presti, Gary Goss, James Wilson, Susie Labry, Kenny Gill and Tillman Franks.

The group is shown performing at a "Couchon de Lait" (Cajun for pig roast) in Mansura, LA in 1992. Left to right are James Wilson, Gov. Davis, Anna Davis and Kenny Gill.

The Jimmie Davis Singers are shown at the Jimmie Davis Homecoming at Beech Springs, LA in 1993. Left to right are James Wilson, Anna Davis, Gov. Davis, Kenny Gill and Gary Goss.

Gov. Jimmie Davis is shown performing in Washington, D. C. for Alaska Senator Ted Stevens in 1993.

Jimmie Davis is shown performing with the late-great Jimmie Rogers' guitar at his 1997 homecoming at Beech Spring, LA. Shown in the picture are James Wilson, Anna Davis, Gov. Davis and Kenny Gill.

Coleen Templet, Jimmie Davis' long time, faithful secretary, is shown in this 1997 picture.

Friends Susie Labry of Baton Rouge, LA and Country Music Promoter Earl Northrup of Earl's Drive-in in Chaffee, N.Y. are shown at the Jimmie Davis Homecoming at Beech Springs, LA on Oct. 5, 1997.

The famous old Strand Theatre in Shreveport, LA is where Gov. Davis's film Louisiana held its world premier in 1947. In 1997, Gov. Davis was there again with Merle Haggard for a 98th Birthday Celebration.

This is a scene from Gov. Davis' 98th Birthday Party at the Strand Theatre in Shreveport, LA Left to right are Gary Goss, James Wilson, unidentified, Johnny Presti, Gov. Davis, Ted Jones, Rob Nash, and Kenny Gill.

Mr. and Mrs. Merle Haggard, are shown with Gov. Davis and Shelby Singleton at the Governor's 98th Birthday Party in 1997.

BlueCross BlueShield
of Louisiana
An independent licensee of the Blue Cross
and Blue Shield Association.

98th Birthday Celebration

HONORING
GOVERNOR JIMMIE DAVIS

STARRING
MERLE HAGGARD

And The Shreveport
Louisiana Hayride.
featuring
The Tillman Franks Singers
Maggie Lewis Warwick
Gordon Kennedy — Grammy Winner, Song
of the Year-"Change The World" By Eric Clapton
Bryan Kennedy — Garth Brooks Show-
Writer of The Hit "Beaches of Cheyenne"
and The Louisiana Hayride Band

Gordon & Bryan Kennedy

LOUISIANA
HAYRIDE
"Cradle of the Stars"

SEPTEMBER 11, 1997 • 7:00 p.m.
The Strand Theatre • Shreveport, LA

Ticket Prices: $16.50, $26.50, $31.50   Sponsored by the FAME Foundation of Shreveport- Bossier, Inc.

Poster announcing Gov. Davis' 98th Birthday Celebration on Sept. 11, 1997.

Gov. Jimmie Davis and the late country music singer Johnny Horton are shown at a show in Bunkie, LA, in 1954.

Kenny Gill in 1947, at the age of 11, in his hometown of Bunkie, LA.

Kenny Gill in a 1962 photo.

Kenny Gill is shown performing with the Baton Rouge, LA. Symphony in 1979.

Kenny Gill was inducted into the Louisiana Music Hall of Fame in Lafayette, LA. on April 13, 1997. He is shown with President Lou Gabbus.

Jeanene and Kenny Gill are shown with long-time friend and highly respected WSM Grand Ole Opry Photographer Les Leverett of Nashville, TN.

NASHVILLE, TENNESSEE

KENNY GILL

Kenny Gill's versatile guitar talent has graced the live performances and recording sessions of a virtual who's who of notable music greats from Al Hirt to Glen Campbell. The mellow tones of his guitar are always sweet whether he's playing Country, Pop, Jazz, Big Band or Rhythm & Blues. Kenny's long and stellar career began with a love of the guitar at age seven. At age 13, he was playing the guitar as a regular on local radio programs in his home town of Bunkie, Louisiana.

A legendary jazz guitarist, Kenny formed the *Kenny Gill Quartet* more than 25 years ago. His first album, *"Guitar Moods of Kenny Gill + 2"* was recorded at the famous New Orleans recording studio, Cosimo Studios, in 1962. This album has recently been re-mastered and re-released and is entitled *"The Original Kenny Gill Trio."* Quite a country picker as well, Kenny Gill has performed and toured with Governor Jimmy Davis since 1972. Kenny records and performs in Nashville frequently and has performed on the *Grand Ole Opry*.

Kenny Gill is a world class guitarist whose style and technique is legendary among musicians. He was recently honored for his many contributions to the world of music by being inducted into the **Louisiana Music Hall of Fame.**

JIMMIE H. DAVIS
BATON ROUGE, LA. 70802
1331 LAKERIDGE DRIVE

A LETTER OF RECOMENDATION

Mr.Kenny Gill has been my guitarist and close friend for
the past 25 years. He is a very dependable and trustworthy
person able to perform any style of music from country to
Jazz. His talents on guitar are very wide and varied,I
highly recomend Kenny's abillities whether it be
performing shows,sessions or any other needs you have for
a top notch guitarist,Kenny can do it all.

Very truly yours,

Jimmie Davis
Former Governor of Louisiana

A WORD FROM HIS FRIENDS

"His talents on guitar are very wide and varied, I highly recommend Kenny's abilities whether it be performing shows or recording sessions, he's a topnotch guitarist, Kenny can do it all."

Former Governor Jimmie Davis of Louisiana

"Kenny is probably one of the most natural guitarists I've worked with. When he plays it sounds like it's coming from his heart, he never overplays. Every note means something. He's a great soloist, a fine rhythm player, a great session player, and I guess the greatest compliment I can pay him is to say he's a very professional person."

Pianist, Ronnie Kole – New Orleans

When asked how he enjoyed Kenny Gill sitting in with his band at a performance in Baton Rouge, his answer was: "All I can say is who taught that man how to boogie."

Clarence "Gatemouth" Brown

"I've just always thought Kenny was the most versatile, most professional, most polished guitarist I've ever met and I've met a lot of them. Besides that, he's just a really nice guy and a good friend."

Rod Bernard – KLFY TV

"My good friend Kenny, what a great picker".

Jett Williams

"His achievements came about solely through his own efforts and hard work. We are proud of our Bunkie native son."

Mayor Fred Feeney – Bunkie, Louisiana

Louisiana Hall Of Fame

INDUCTS

Kenny Gill

ON THIS _____ 13th _____ DAY OF _____ April _____ 199Z.

Kenny Gill has been described as a man of many talents, being a licensed pilot, electronic technician, amateur radio operator, notary and musician, however music has always been paramount in his life. The KENNY GILL MODERN JAZZ QUARTET was formed about 25 years ago and has enjoyed much success. Gill has performed with such greats as JACK JONES, VIC DIMONNE, ROD BERNARD, DALE & GRACE, JIMMY DICKENS, JERRY LEE LEWIS, JOHNNY PRESTON, JOHNNY HORTON, HANK WILLIAMS JR., JIMMY CLANTON, CONWAY TWITTY and GOVERNOR JIMMIE DAVIS for the past 25 years. Gill has five albums to his credit, "FASCINATING GUITAR", "THE KENNY GILL GUITAR IN SESSION". "KENNY GILL PLUS TWO", "COOL GUITAR" and "KENNY GILL PICKS ON SINATRA" plus three singles, "GOLDEN ANGEL / PLASTER OF PARIS", "MARY ANN / PLEDGING MY LOVE", "FREDDIE MAE 1&2". Gill performed at the GRAND OLE OPRY, THE LOUISIANA HAYRIDE, THE NEW ORLEANS JAZZ FESTIVAL, MANY TELEVISION SHOWS AND LIVE RADIO PROGRAMS. GILL IS CREDITED FOR HIS OUTSTANDING TECHNICAL ARRANGEMENT ON DALE & GRACES' number one hit "IM LEAVING IT UP TO YOU", then subsequently became their road manager and musical director. Gill, a world class guitars whose "all encompassing" style and technique are legendary among musicians. On July 12, 1996, Gill was invited to perform at the annual CHET ATKINS APPRECIATION CELEBRATION in Nashville, TN which attracts noted guitarists from around the world.

Kathleen Babineaux Blanco
LIEUTENANT GOVERNOR

Lou Gabus
PRESIDENT & FOUNDER

THE

JIMMIE DAVIS SINGERS AWARD

PRESENTED TO

KENNY GILL

In recognition of many years of musical support and friendship. This award also recognizes and affirms the continued dependability and enthusiasm of the recipient.

Jimmie Davis

Governor Jimmie H. Davis   SEPT. 11, 1997

87

KENNY GILL

**PERFORMED OR
RECORDED WITH:**

Jack Jones
Phyllis Diller
Vic DiMonne
Snooky Lansen
Dave Gardner
Jimmie Davis
Rod Bernard
Joy Lansing
Hommer & Jethro
Ronnie Kole
Dale & Grace
Jimmy C. Newman
Jimmy Dickens
Owen Bradley
Jerry Lee Lewis
Bob Wills
Jivin Gene
Johnny Preston
Al Hirt
Carmen Cavalaro
Don Cherry
Tillman Franks
Johnny Horton
Tex Ritter
April Stevens
Chuck Wagon Gang
Boots Randolph
Pete Fountain
Hank Locklin
Johnny Russell
Johnny Gimble
Benny Barnes
Buck Rogers
Jimmy Clanton
Bobby Goldsboro
Bobby Rydell
Doug Kershaw
Glenn Campbell

Geo. "Goober" Linsey
Minnie Pearl
Billy Grammer
Hank Williams Jr.
Conway Twitty
Red Sovine
George Burns
Leroy Van Dyke
Jerry Van Dyke
Dale Houston
Benny Spellman
Warner Mack
Baton Rouge Symphony
Bill Conti
Gatemouth Brown
Mark Dinning
Johnny Tillitson
The Ames Brothers
Lonzo & Oscar
Jack Greene
Cal Smith
Jett Williams
Charlie Walker
Hager Twins
Merle Kilgore
Claude King
Paul Howard

ALBUMS:
Fascinating Guitar
Kenny Gill in Session
Kenny Gill Plus Two
Kenny Gill Cool Guitar
Kenny Gill Picks on Sinatra
Kenny Gill Christmas Guitar
Kenny Gill Solo Guitar
Kenny Gill A Tribute to Chet

RECORDED FOR:

Mercury Records
Paula Records
Word Records
Michelle Records
Starday Records
Jim Records
Swallow Records
Big Cloud Records
Carl Records
Jin Records
Lanor Records
Montel Redords

PERFORMED AT:

Grand Ole Opry
Louisiana Hayride
New Orleans Jazz Festival
Chet Atkins Apprec. Society
Chet Atkins Musician Week
TV and Radio Shows
Club Acts

MEMBER OF:
Louisiana Music
Hall of Fame

Nashville Local 257

Reunion of Professional
Entertainers

Mister Guitar

The Chet Atkins Appreciation Society Newsletter

Issue 39   October 1996

The Kenny Gill Quartet from Baton Rouge did a lounge set featuring *Beginning to See the Light, Days of Wine and Roses, From Out of Nowhere, give Me the Happy Life,* and closed with Bill Spann's request for *Stars Fell On Alabama*

KENNY GILL

Kenny is a veteran of the Nashville scene. He is comfortable with many styles of guitar playing. He is gracious to bring his band and perform for us.

AMERICAN MUSIC
MAGAZINE

NR. 75 • MARS • 1998

AMERICAN MUSIC MAGAZINE
FLINTGATAN 16 • S-432 35 VARBERG • SWEDEN • TEL INT + 46-34018645 • FAX INT + 46-34087724

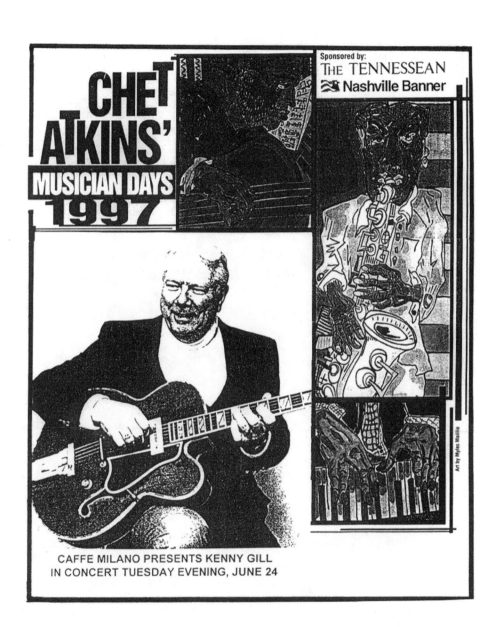

CHET ATKINS' MUSICIAN DAYS 1997

Sponsored by:
THE TENNESSEAN
Nashville Banner

Art by Myles Maillie

CAFFE MILANO PRESENTS KENNY GILL
IN CONCERT TUESDAY EVENING, JUNE 24

FEBRUARY 1997
VOLUME 1 ISSUE 5

FREE

Baton Rouge

GOOD TIMES

THE ENTERTAINMENT AUTHORITY

Kenny Gill

a lifetime of music

INSIDE: The Most Complete Live Entertainment Listings Available

GUITAR LEGEND

KENNY GILL

Kenny Gill-Nashville, TN

IN CONCERT

PLACE _____

DATE _____

Member of the Louisiana Music Hall Of Fame

Personal appearance poster.

If you enjoy good guitar music whether it's country, jazz, big band, gospel or thumb picking, Kenny Gill has recorded it. And you can purchase it on our website at www.kennygill.com or write to us at Papillon Records, P.O. Box 1191, Mt. Juliet, TN 37122. We would like to hear from you.

Thank you,
Papillon Records